Cell Biology
7th Grade Textbook
Children's Biology Books

BABY PROFESSOR

EDUCATION KIDS

Speedy Publishing LLC
40 E. Main St. #1156
Newark, DE 19711
www.speedypublishing.com
Copyright 2016

What are you made of? There is a world inside you. But you can't see this world without the help of a microscope!

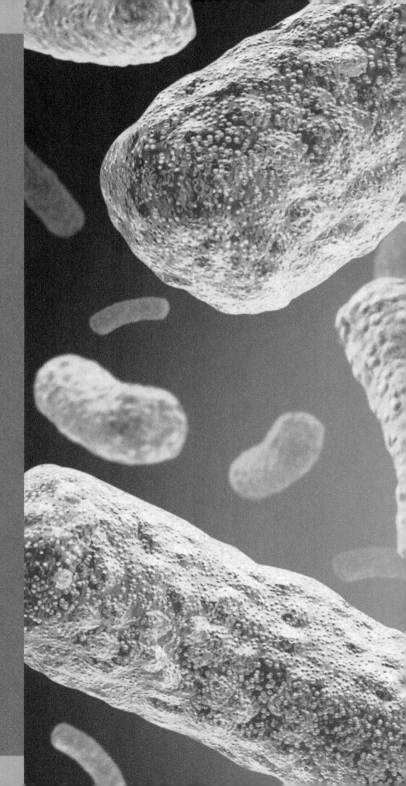

You are made up of billions of cells. You have a world of cells inside your body. These tiny units form together to make all the parts of your body.

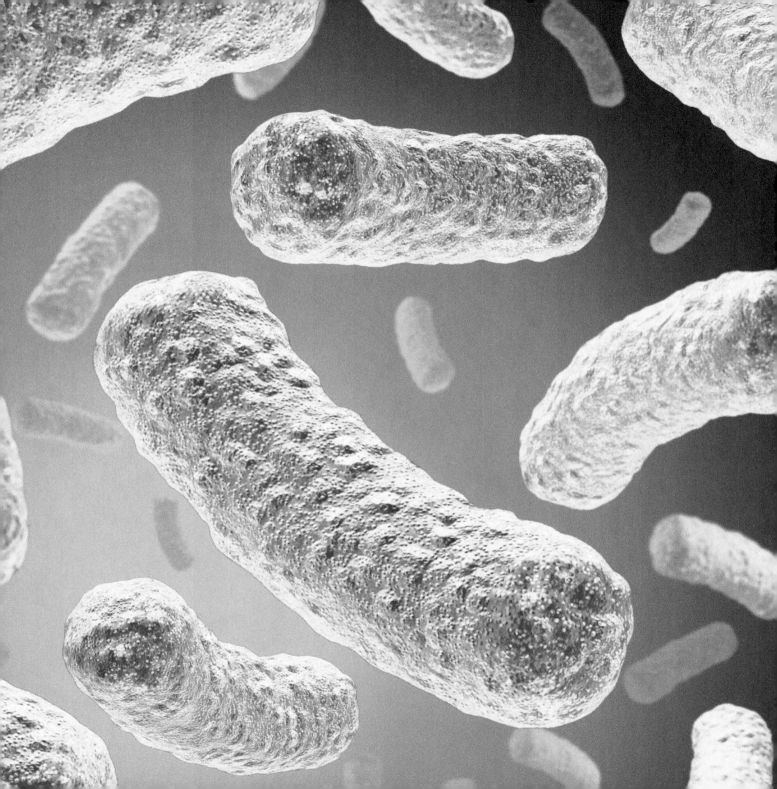

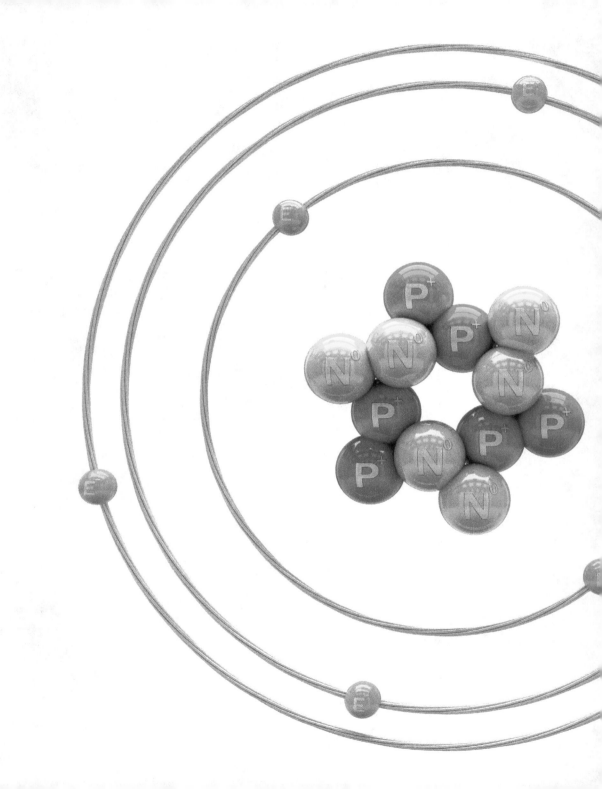

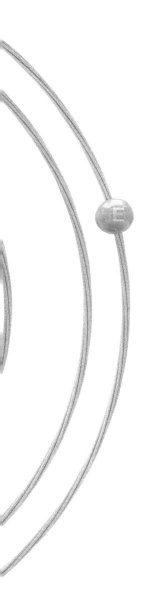

Cells are the basic units of life. The word cell is of Latin origin. It comes from the word cellula, which means a small compartment.

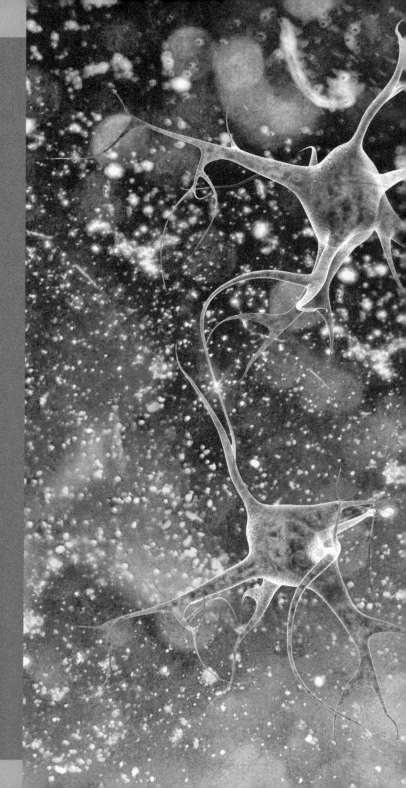

All living things are made up of cells. Even the tiniest organisms in the world have cells. Bacteria are made up a single cell each. Some organisms are made up of trillions of cells. We are made up of cells.

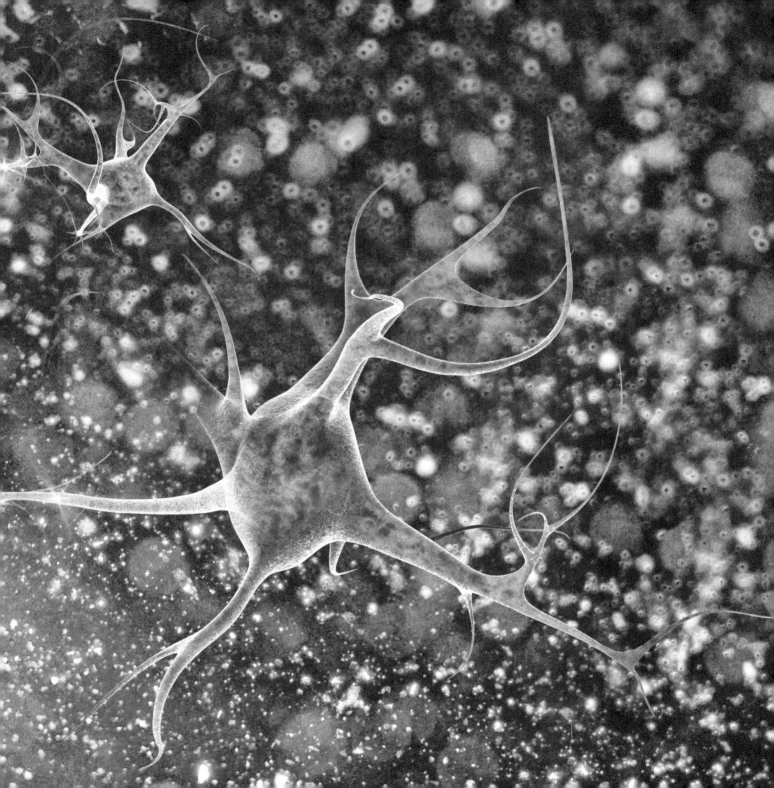

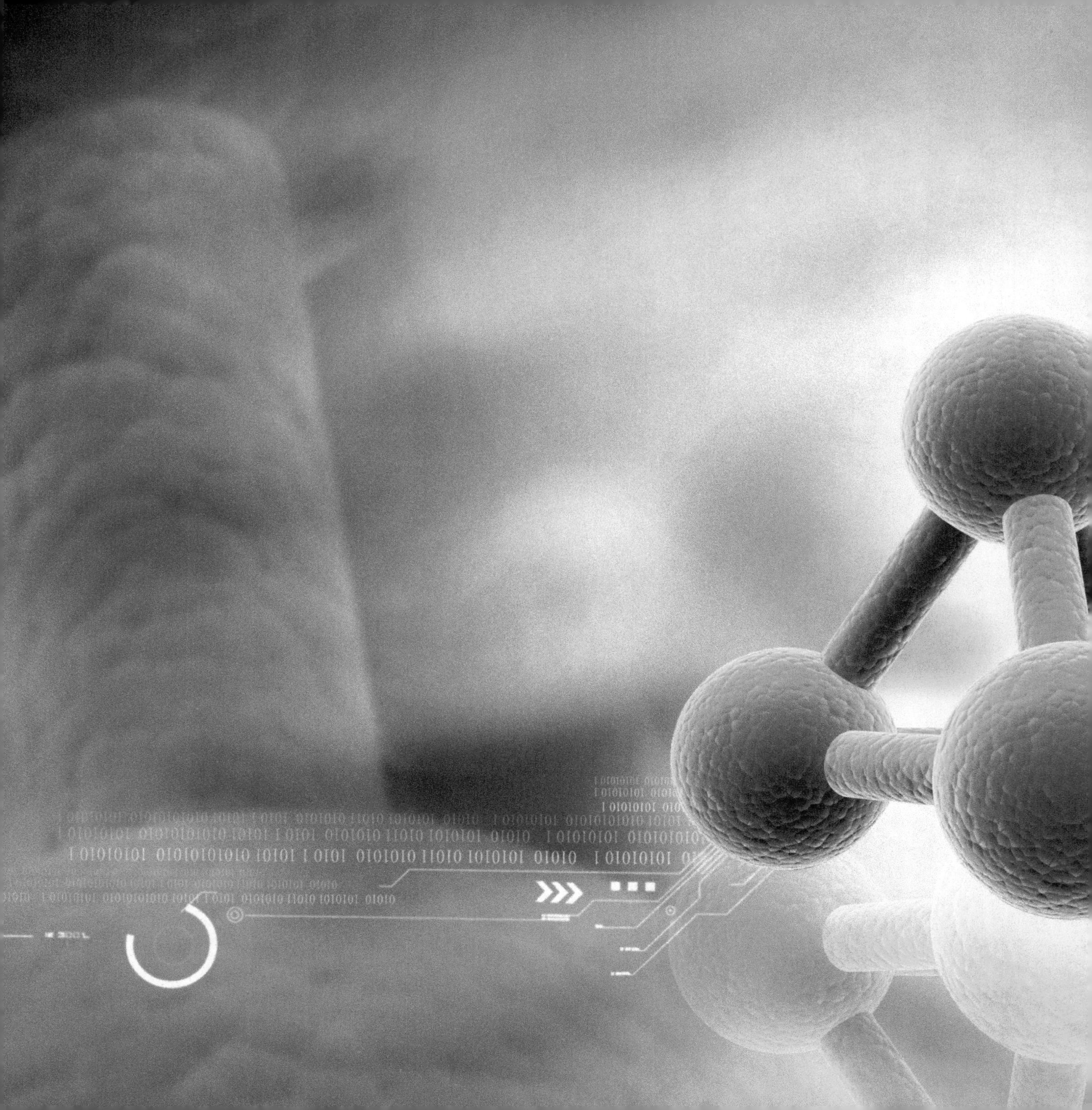

Welcome to the world of cells!

Did you know that the human body carries more bacteria cells than human cells? This is sort of odd to think about!

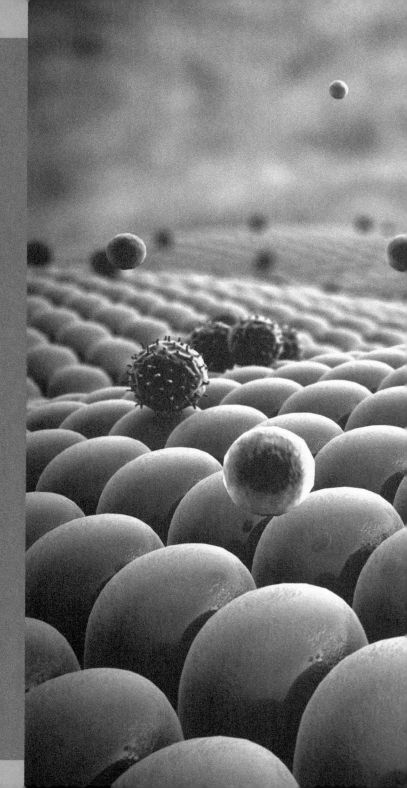

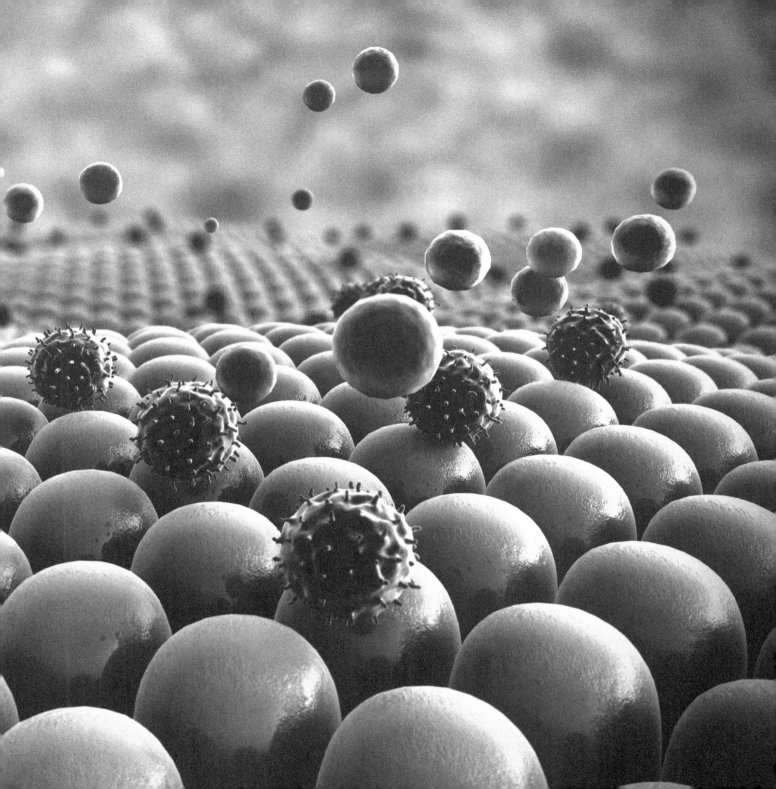

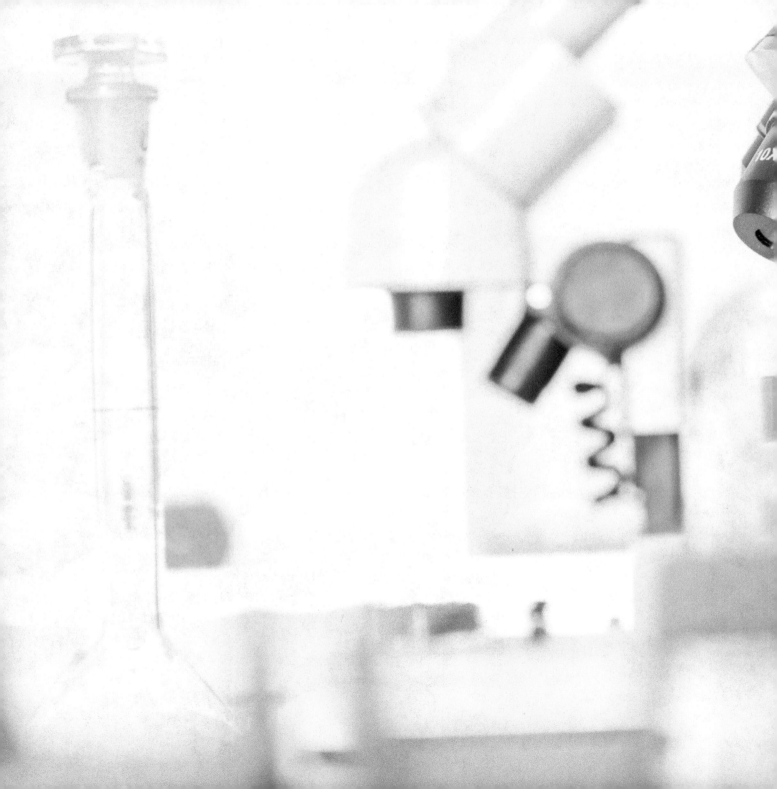

Cells were discovered by the scientist Robert Hooke. The ostrich egg is one of the largest known cells. It weighs more than three pounds. When cells are in group they form a tissue.

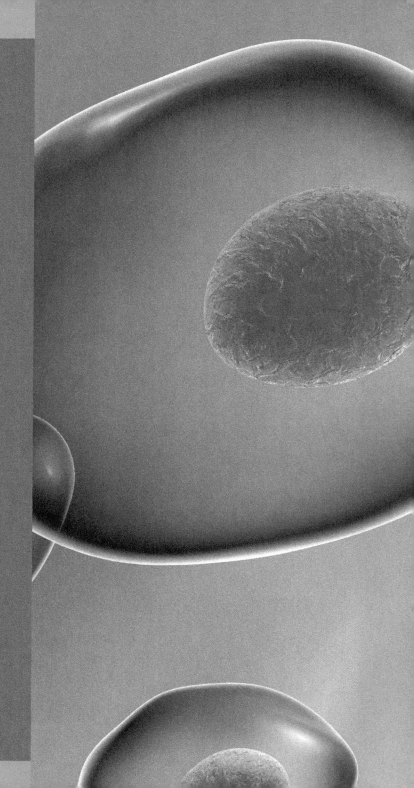

What is Cell Biology? It is a scientific field that studies cells and their functions. Scientists who study cells are known as cell biologists. They study the structure and functions of cells. They observe how cells work.

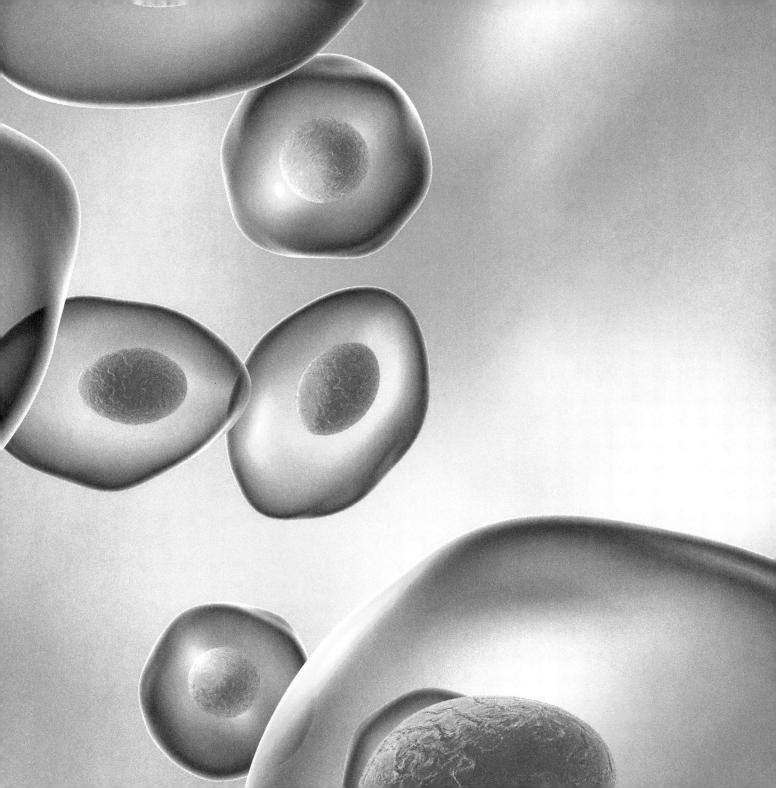

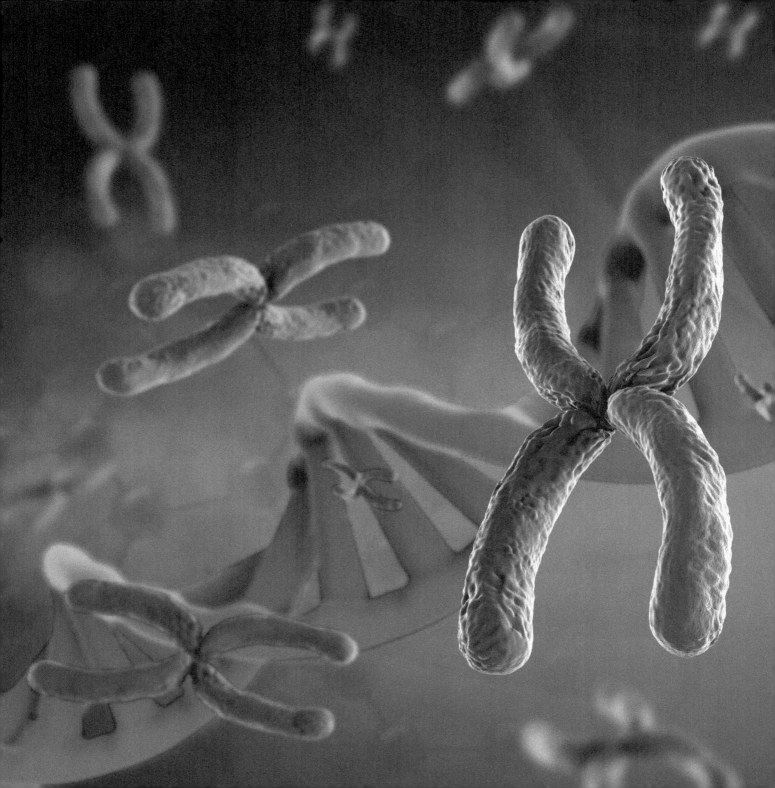

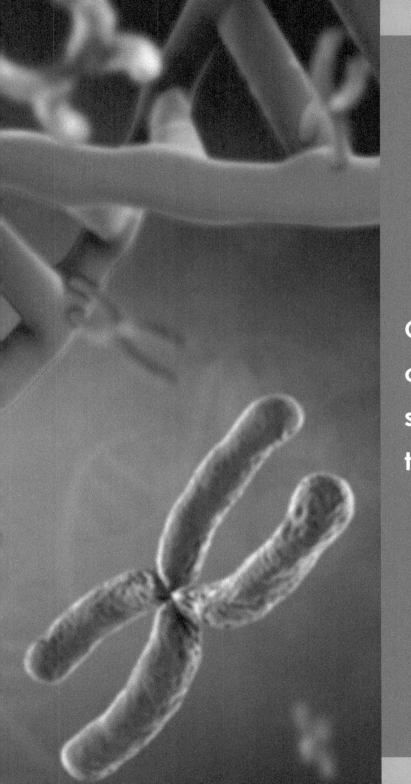

Our body has nerve
cells. They send
signals and messages
to the entire body.

We have the ability to think and make important decisions because of our tiny brain cells. We are able to move around because of the help of our muscle cells.

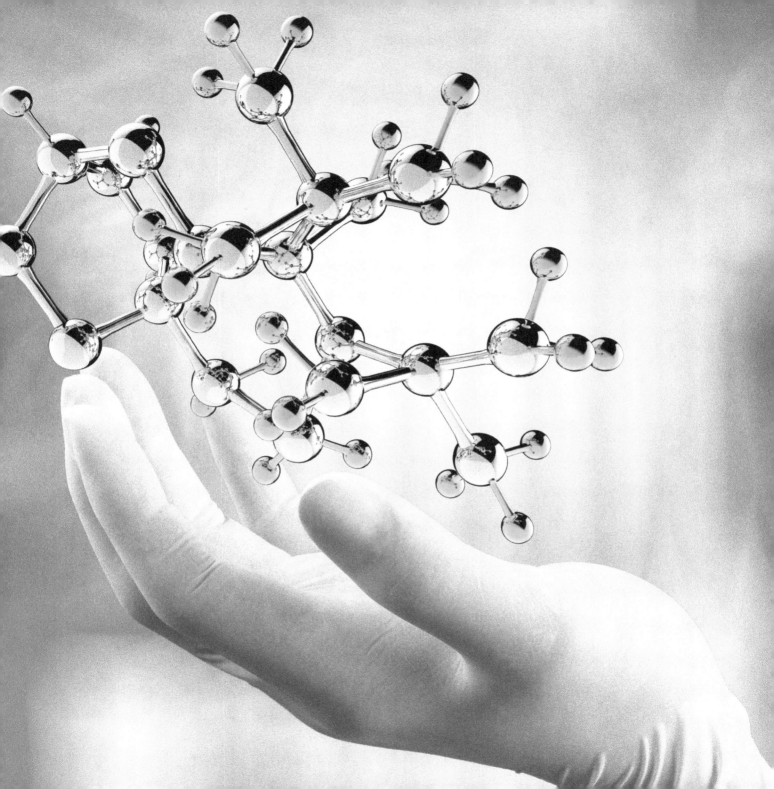

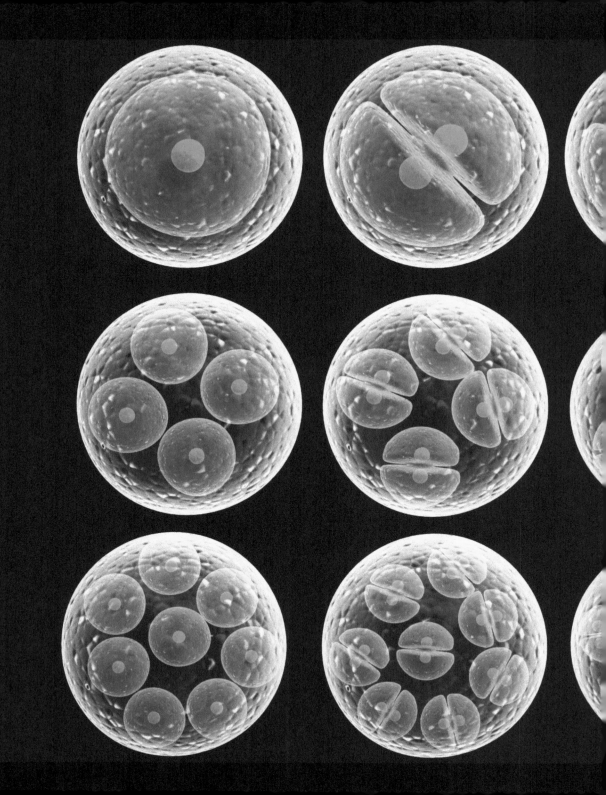

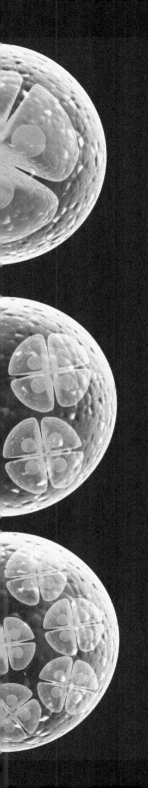

Amazingly, our body parts perform different functions to keep us alive because of our cells. Each type of cell differs from the others. Each type has different functions.

TWO MAIN
CATEGORIES OF CELLS

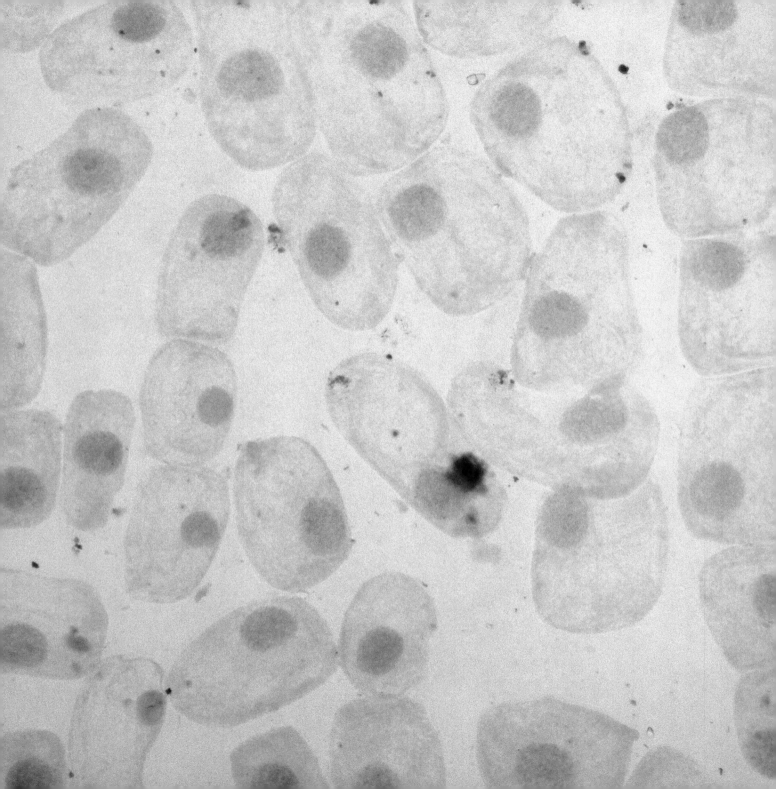

**Prokaryotic Cells-
These cells contain
no nucleus. They are
the small and simple
cells. Bacteria are
organisms which
are made up of
prokaryotic cells.**

Three main parts of a prokaryotic cell:

Outside Protection (cell wall, membrane, and the capsule).

Flagella – They are little whips that help the cell move. Not all cells have flagella.

Cytoplasmic Region- this is the inside of the cell. It contains the nucleoid, cytoplasm, and ribosomes.

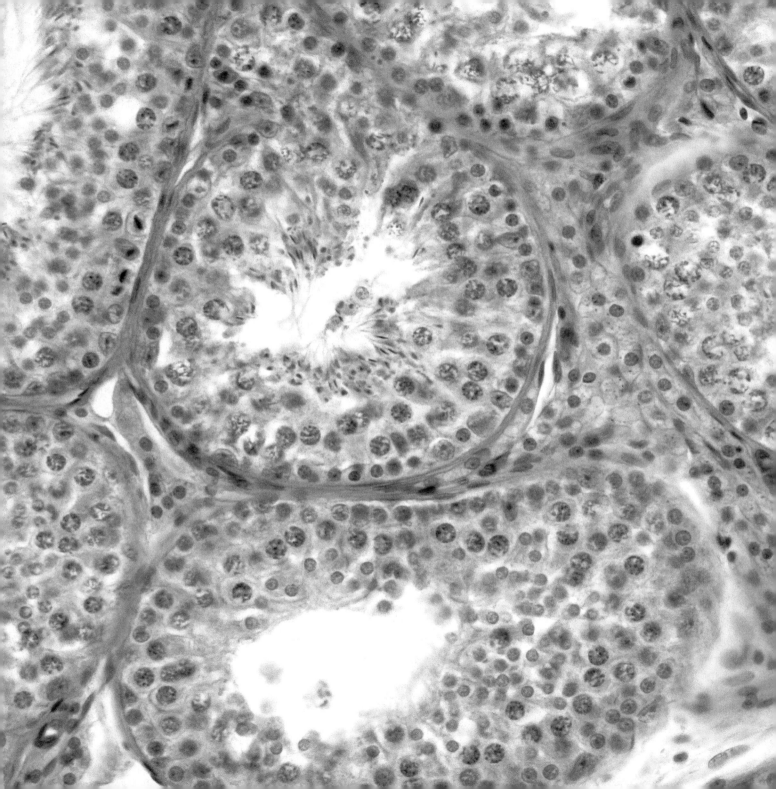

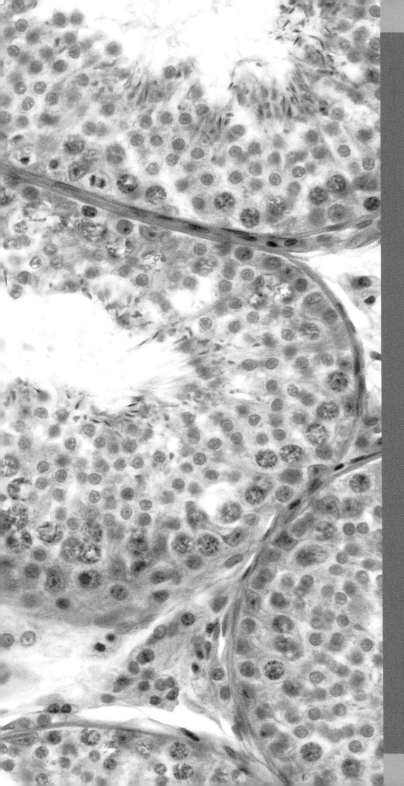

Eukaryotic Cells-
These are complex
and bigger cells.
They are complex
cells. They have
a definite nucleus
which contains the
DNA of the cell.
Eukaryotic cells
are found in plants
and animals.

MAIN COMPONENTS
OF MOST CELLS

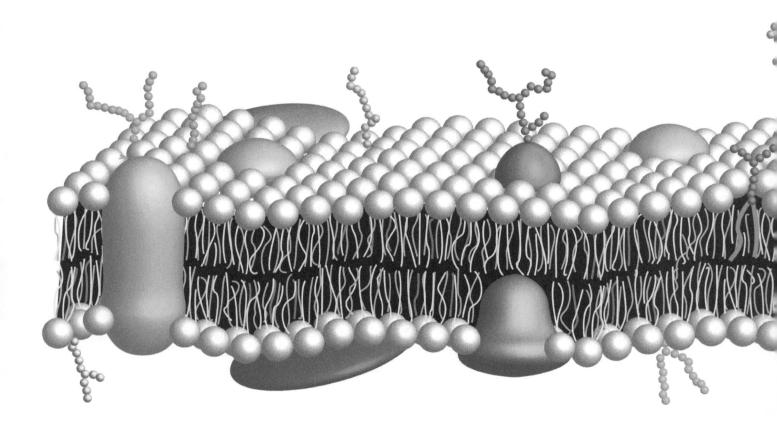

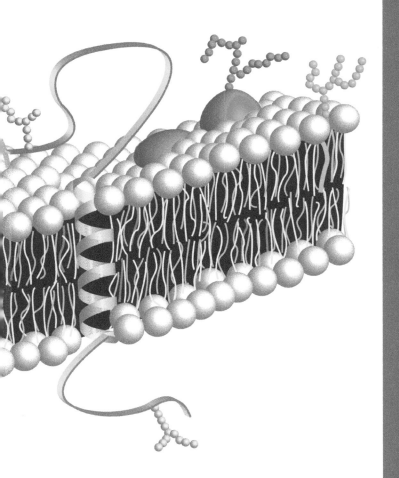

Membrane - This is the covering of the cell. It serves as the "skin" of the cell. It's the outer part of the cell. It accepts and sends out substances.

A cell membrane is found in both plant and animal cells. However, in plant cells, the cell membrane is the second wall. It is found inside the main cell wall. Plant cell walls are thick. They make the cells stronger.

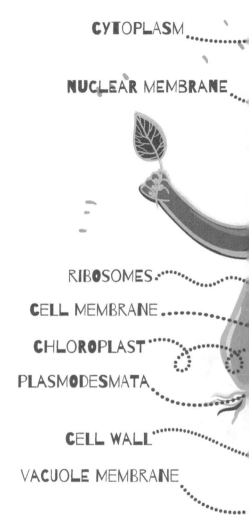

CYTOPLASM

NUCLEAR MEMBRANE

RIBOSOMES

CELL MEMBRANE

CHLOROPLAST

PLASMODESMATA

CELL WALL

VACUOLE MEMBRANE

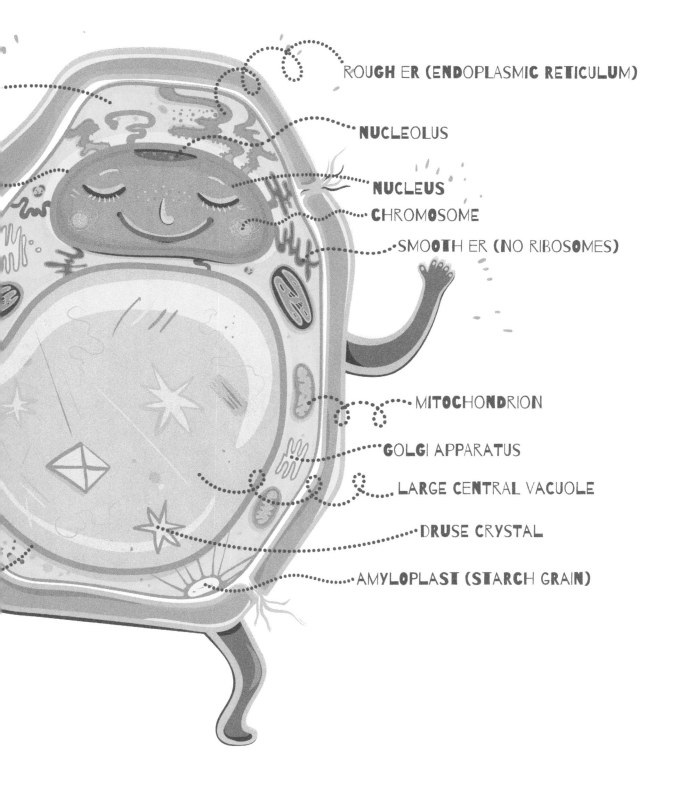

ROUGH ER (ENDOPLASMIC RETICULUM)

NUCLEOLUS

NUCLEUS

CHROMOSOME

SMOOTH ER (NO RIBOSOMES)

MITOCHONDRION

GOLGI APPARATUS

LARGE CENTRAL VACUOLE

DRUSE CRYSTAL

AMYLOPLAST (STARCH GRAIN)

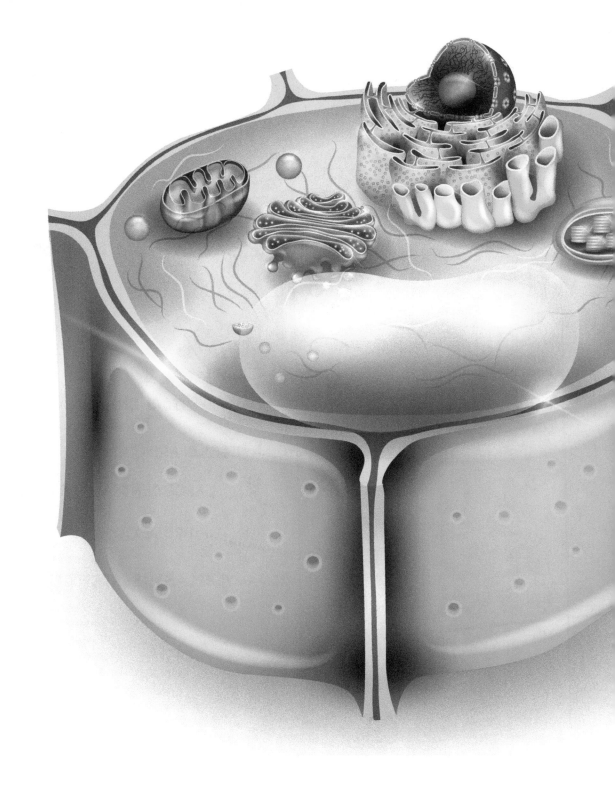

Cell walls are found only in plant cells and not in animal cells. Cell walls are made from cellulose. These strong cells let the plants grow tall and strong.

The cell membranes of animals contain cholesterol. This is what makes the membrane harder. On the other hand, plants don't have cholesterol. Instead they have the cell wall. Hence, the cell membranes of plants are softer.

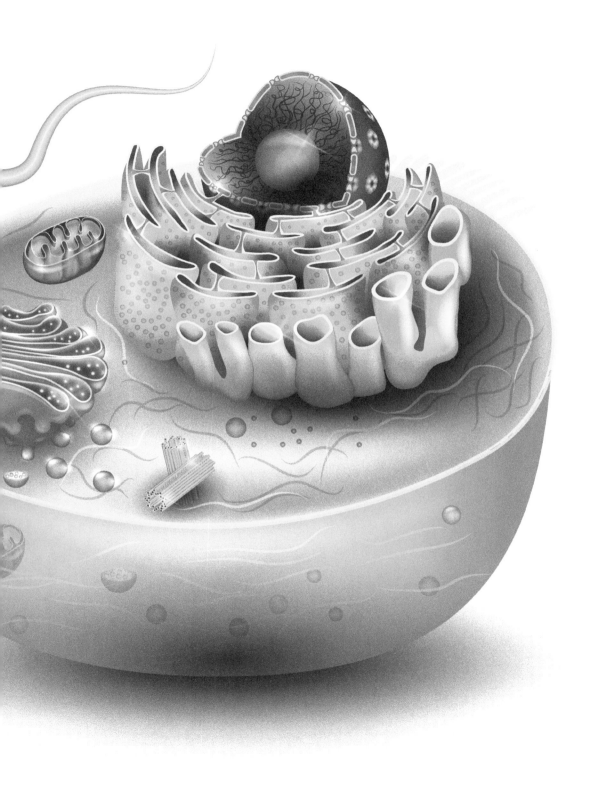

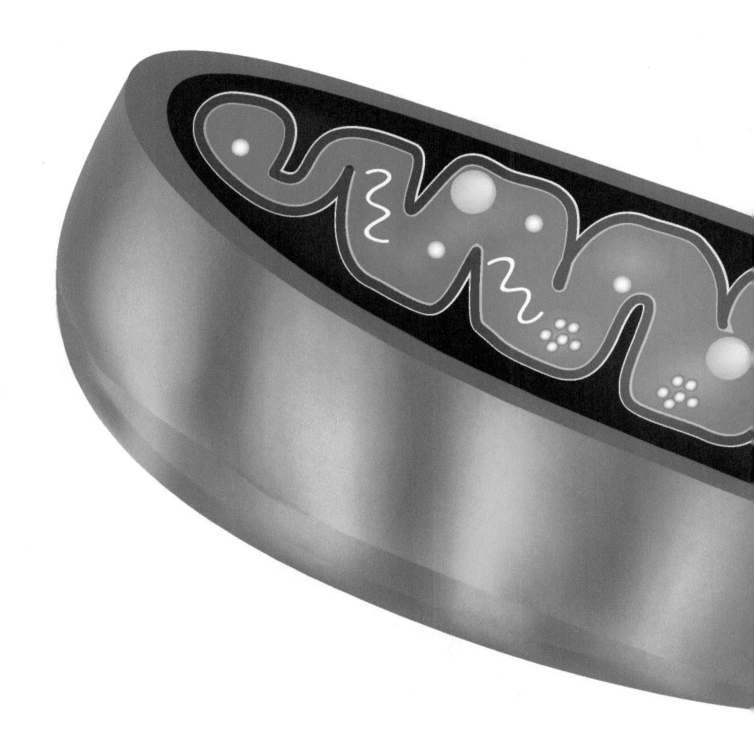

Mitochondria - This is the cell's source of energy. It's where our digested food reacts with oxygen to create energy for the cell.

Ribosomes - They produce what the cells need in order to function. Ribosomes act as factories of the needs of the cells. This is where proteins are formed.

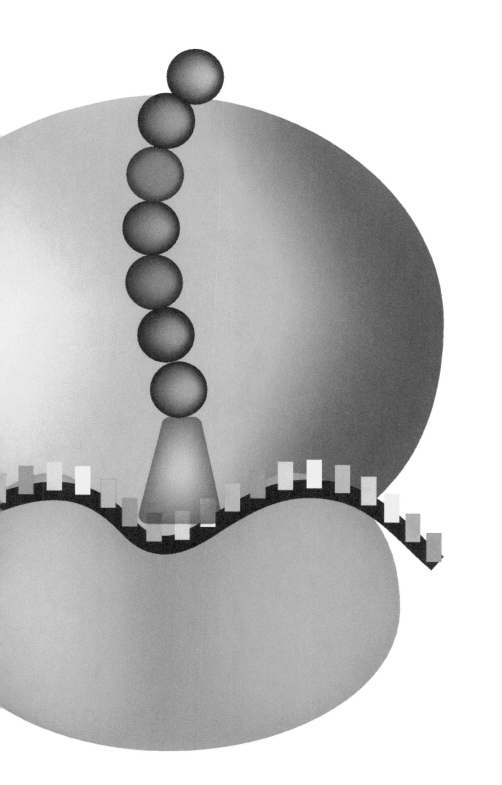

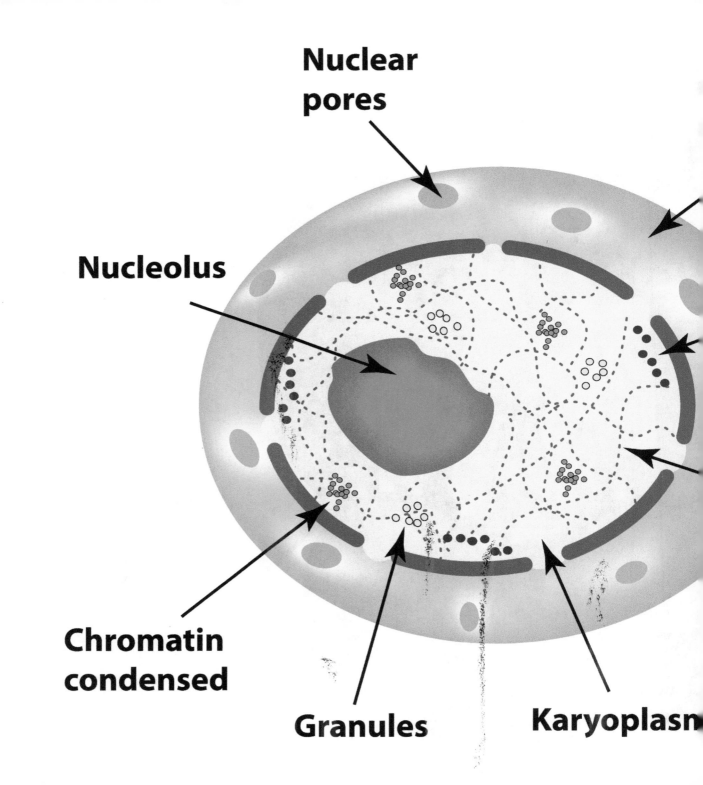

Nuclear pores

Nucleolus

Chromatin condensed

Granules

Karyoplasm

**ear
brane**

Fibrils

**Chromatin
diffuse**

Nucleus - It acts
as the brain of the
cell. This region uses
chromosomes to
give instructions to
the rest of the cell.

Cytoplasm - It is mostly water. It is the component for the rest of the cell.

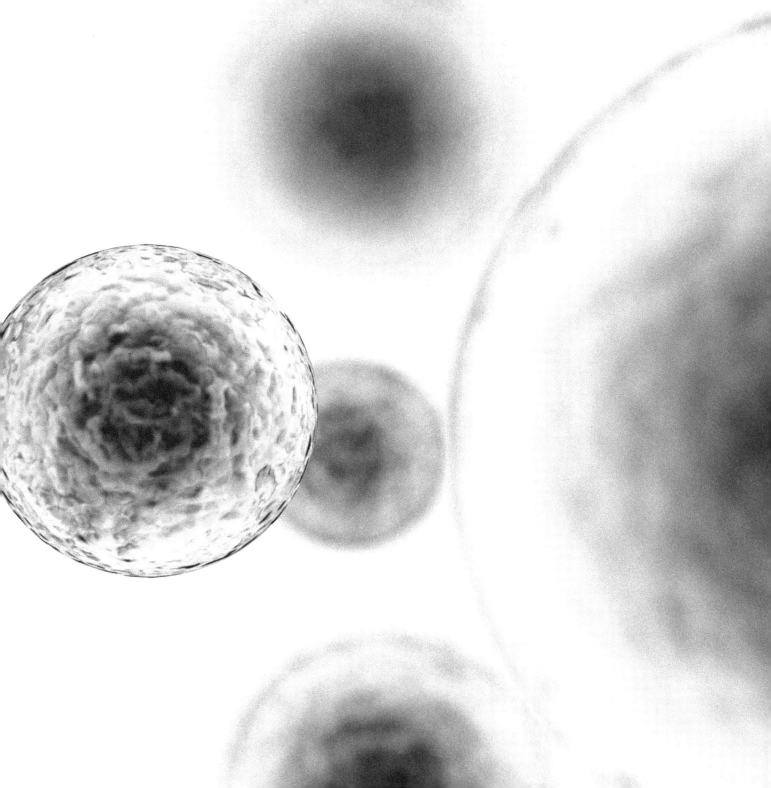

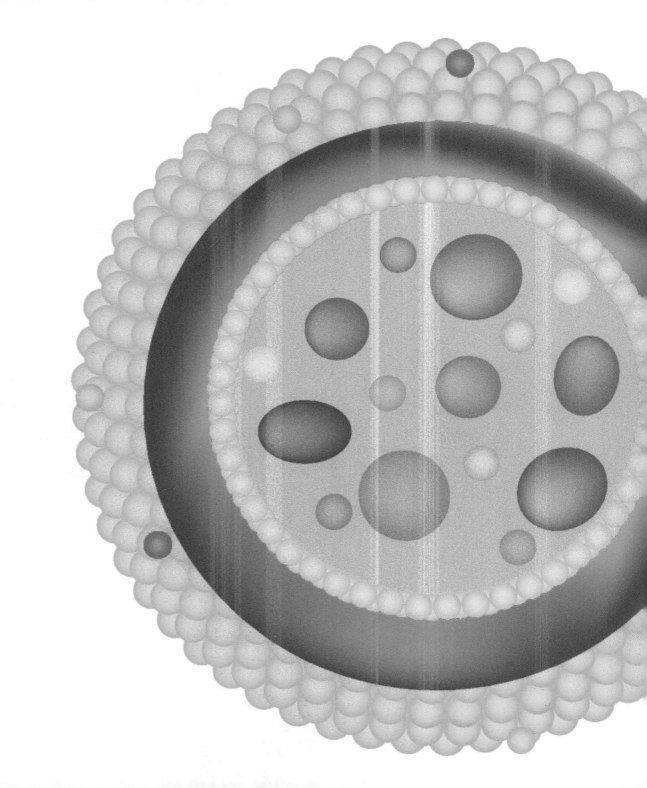

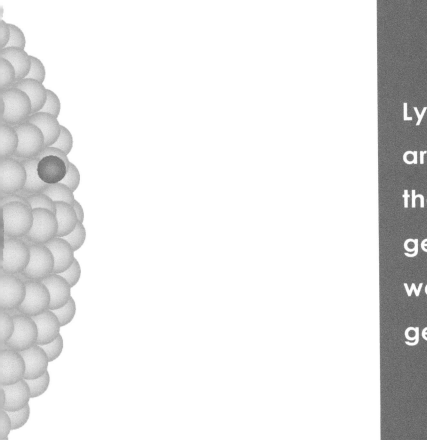

Lysosomes - These are the cleaners of the cell. Lysosomes get rid of the waste that may get into the cell.

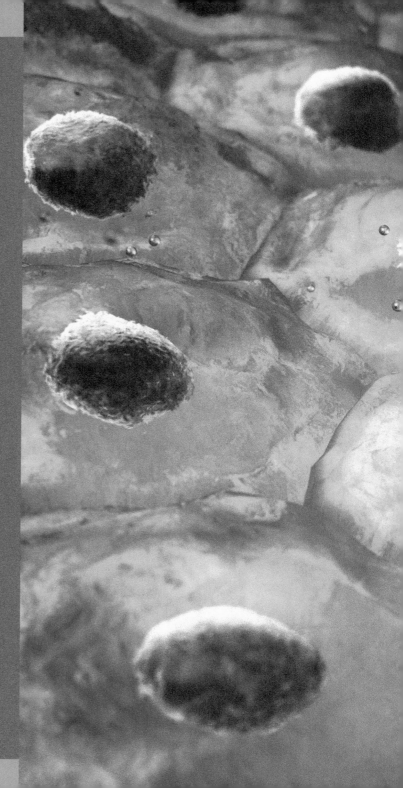

Organelles refer to the nucleus, ribosomes, and lysosomes. These are the tiny organisms inside the cell.

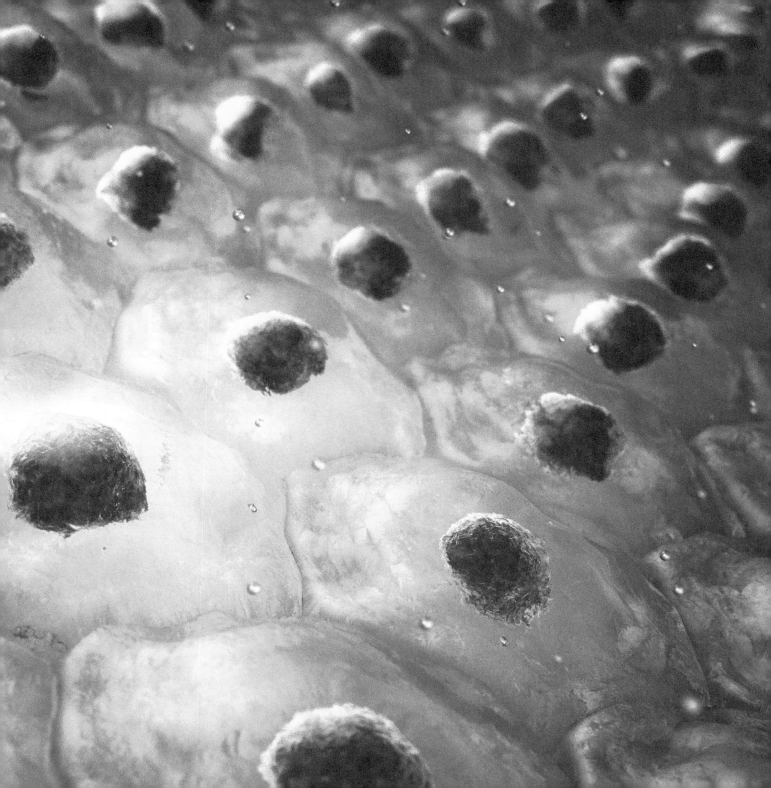

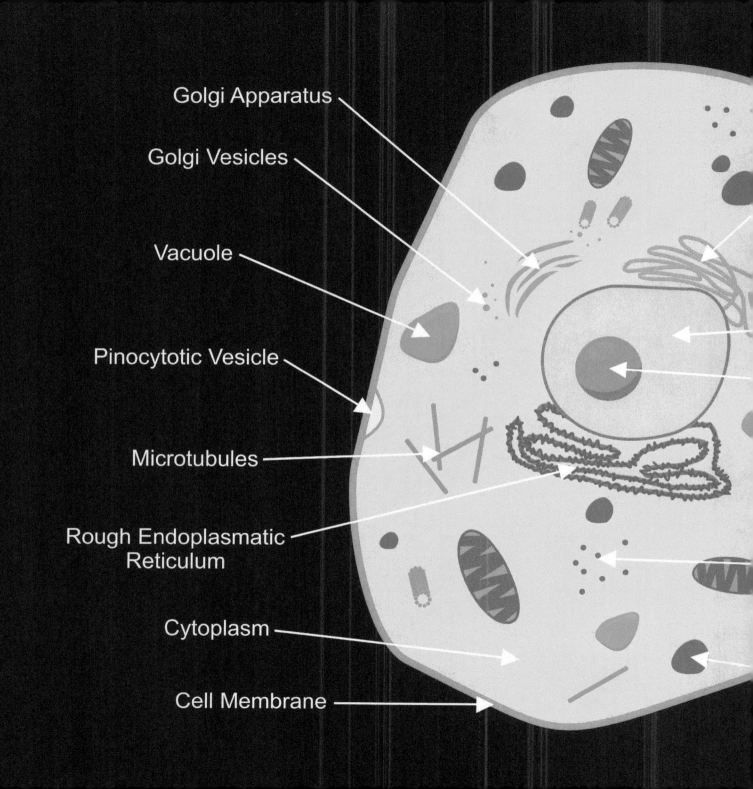

Golgi Apparatus

Golgi Vesicles

Vacuole

Pinocytotic Vesicle

Microtubules

Rough Endoplasmatic
Reticulum

Cytoplasm

Cell Membrane

Smooth Endoplasmatic
Reticulum

Mitochondrion

Nucleus

Nucleolus

Centrioles

Ribosomes

Lysosome

Organelle means
a small organ. The
nucleus, ribosomes,
and lysosomes are
the main organs
of the cell.

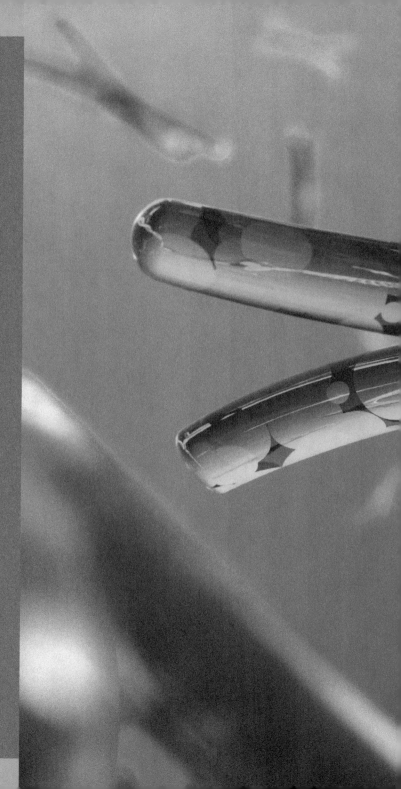

They provide the needs of the cell. Organelles keep the cells alive. The organelles work very hard to provide food for the cells, to protect the cells from unwanted substances, and to perform other functions.

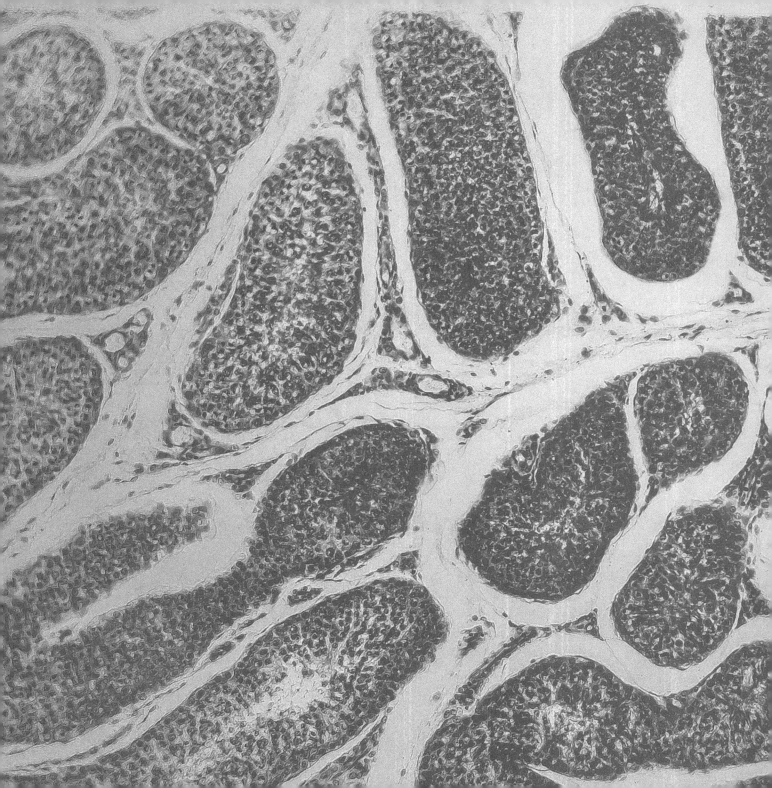

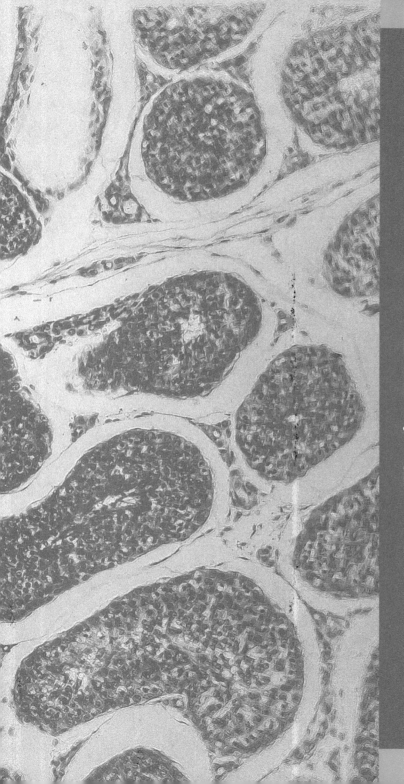

Cells grow and reproduce. They multiply. All living things need cells in order to grow.

Therefore, cells work hard to multiply themselves to support our growing needs. New cells have to be made to repair damaged areas of the body. Most cells multiply by duplicating the material inside of them.

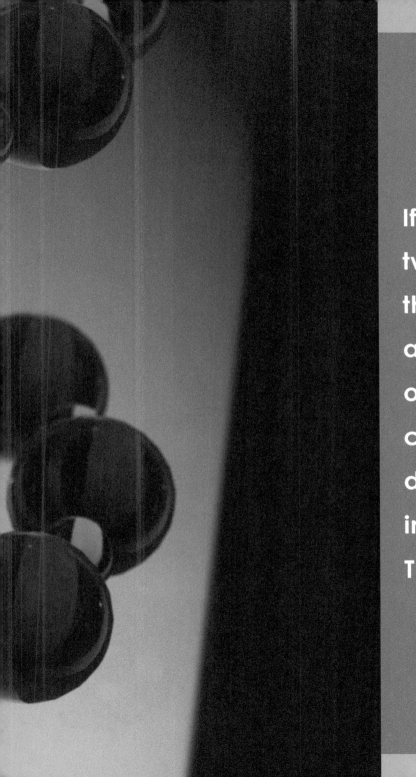

If a cell breaks into two, it undergoes the process known as mitosis. On the other hand, some cells, like germ cells, divide themselves into four new cells. This is called meiosis.

CPSIA information can be obtained
at www.ICGtesting.com
Printed in the USA
BVHW012205270320
576248BV00012B/355

9 781541 905443